# Crazy eights

## AND OTHER CARD GAMES

By **Joanna Cole**
and **Stephanie Calmenson**

Illustrated by
**Alan Tiegreen**

**SeaStar Books**

NEW YORK

SEASTAR BOOKS
A division of NORTH-SOUTH BOOKS INC.

Published in the United States in 2002 by SeaStar Books, a division of North-South Books Inc., New York.
Published simultaneously in Great Britain, Canada, Australia, and New Zealand by North-South Books,
an imprint of Nord-Süd Verlag AG, Gossau Zürich, Switzerland.

Library of Congress Cataloging-in-Publication Data
Cole, Joanna.
Crazy eights and other card games/by Joanna Cole
and Stephanie Calmenson; illustrated by Alan Tiegreen.
p. cm.
Summary: Introduces the different suits and face cards
in a deck of cards, explains how to hold, shuffle, and deal them,
and provides instructions for such games as Aces Up, Go Fish, and Spit.
A CIP catalogue record for this book is available from The British Library.
The artwork for this book was prepared by using pen and ink.

ISBN 1-58717-950-4 (reinforced trade edition)
1 3 5 7 9 RTE 10 8 6 4 2
ISBN 1-58717-951-2 (paperback edition)
1 3 5 7 9 PB 10 8 6 4 2

Printed in U.S.A.

For more information about our books, and the authors and artists
who create them, visit our web site: www.northsouth.com

# CONTENTS

# INTRODUCTION

There are many good reasons for playing cards: It's a good way to get together with friends and family. It gives your brain a workout and improves your math skills. It's something to do when there's nothing else to do. And most important, it's fun!

# GETTING TO KNOW THE CARDS
## What's what and who's who in the deck?

There are fifty-two cards in the deck, plus two Jokers. The Jokers are not usually part of a game.

Get to know the cards by sorting them.

**SORT THE CARDS BY COLOR**
There are red cards and black cards.

**SORT THE CARDS BY SUIT**
There are four suits:

**Hearts**          **Diamonds**          **Clubs**          **Spades**

Hearts and Diamonds are always red. Clubs and Spades are always black.

## In each suit, there are thirteen cards:

**Thirteen Hearts**

**Thirteen Diamonds**

**Thirteen Clubs**

**Thirteen Spades**

## SORT THE CARDS BY NUMBER OR LETTER

There are four of each number and letter—one card from each suit:

four Aces    four 2's    four 3's, and so on

Each card has a number or a letter in the corner. The number cards have a number in the corner. Kings, Queens, and Jacks are called *face cards*.

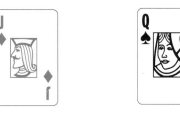

The Jack has a *J*. The Queen has a *Q*. The King has a *K*. The Ace has an *A*.

Each number card has the correct number of Hearts, Diamonds, Spades, or Clubs in the middle of the card.
A 2 of Hearts has two Hearts.
A 3 of Diamonds has three Diamonds.
A 5 of Clubs has five Clubs, and so on.

There are two Jokers. They are used in only a few games. Usually, you take them out of the deck.

# HIGHS AND LOWS

Some cards are higher than others. In a game, a higher card beats a lower card.

Face cards beat number cards.
Kings beat Queens;
Queens beat Jacks;
Jacks beat 10's;
10's beat 9's;
9's beat 8's;
8's beat 7's;
and so on.

In most games, Aces are the highest cards and beat all the other cards. In some games, the Aces are the lowest cards. In other games, Aces can be highest or lowest.

# HOW TO HOLD YOUR CARDS IN A FAN

1. Pick up your cards and hold them in one hand like this:

2. With your other hand, gently move the top card over so you can see the corner of the second card.

3. Then move the first two cards until you see the corner of the third card.

4. Keep doing this until your cards look like this:

If you are left-handed, it will be easier if you start with the cards in your right hand.

## ANOTHER WAY:

Pick up the cards one at a time.

Place them next to each other in your hand to make a fan.

## ANOTHER WAY:

Use an upside-down shoe box to hold your cards for you.

# HOW TO SHUFFLE THE DECK

Every time you play a new game, the dealer must shuffle, or mix, the cards.

**ONE WAY TO SHUFFLE:**
1. Divide the deck into two piles.

2. Hold the piles *loosely*, one above the other.

3. Push the top pile down into the lower pile, mixing the cards.

4. Do this at least three times.

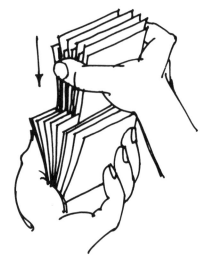

**ANOTHER WAY TO SHUFFLE:**
1. Divide the deck into two piles.

2. Hold each pile this way:

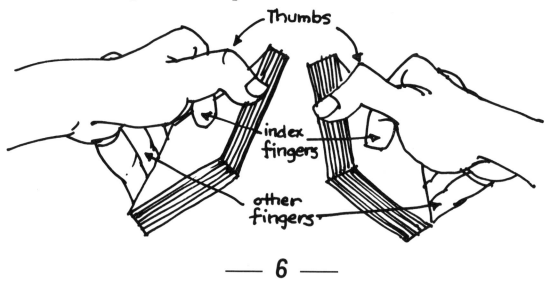

3. Rest your fingers on the table.

4. Gently bend the piles back and use your thumbs to let the cards fall down a few at a time to make a whole deck again.

It may be easier to let the *corners* of piles come together first.

5. Do this at least three times.

**Helpful hint:** For practice, it may be easier to use only part of the pack.

## A THIRD WAY TO SHUFFLE:

1. Spread the deck out on the table.

2. With your hands, slide the cards around so they get all mixed up.

3. Do this about seven times.

# CUTTING THE DECK

To make sure the cards have been shuffled as fairly as possible, the dealer gives one player the chance to rearrange—or cut—the deck.

After shuffling, the dealer presents the pack to the player on his right. The player may cut the pack or pass.

To cut, take cards (at least five) from the top of the pack and place them in a pile face down next to the rest of the pack. The dealer puts the rest of the pack on top of that pile.

To pass, tap the pack.

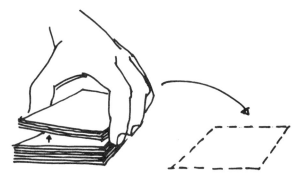

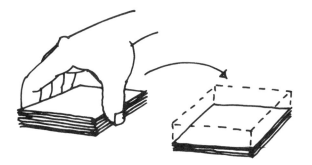

# HOW TO DEAL THE CARDS

First, choose the dealer like this: Each player picks one card from the deck. The player with the highest card is the dealer. (Put the cards back in the deck.)

The dealer shuffles the cards. Then, starting with the top card in the deck, she places one card face down on the table in front of each player, beginning with the person on her left. She keeps dealing cards around to each person until everyone has the correct number of cards.

For the next game, the person on the dealer's left becomes the new dealer.

## WHO GOES FIRST?
The player on the dealer's *left* always makes the first play.

# MAKE A WISH

## This solitaire game tells if your wish will come true.

**Number of players:** One—just you. *Solitaire* means it's a game for *one* player.

**Object of game:** To take away pairs until no cards are left

## SETTING UP THE GAME

♣ Go through the deck. Take out all the 2's, 3's, 4's, 5's, and 6's. You will play with a special deck—with just the cards from 7's to Aces.

Lay these aside.

Use these.

Make a deck.

♣ Using your special deck, count out four cards face up. Make a neat pile so you see only the top card.

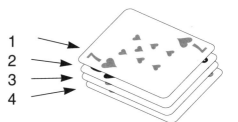

♣ Do this with all the cards. There will be eight piles of four cards each.

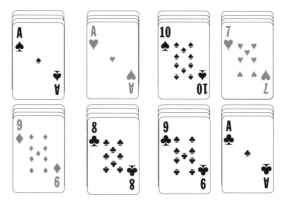

## PLAYING THE GAME

1.  Close your eyes and make a wish.

Play this game by yourself, or take turns with a friend!

2.  Look at the face-up cards. Do you see a pair—two cards that are the same? If you do, pick up both cards and lay them aside.

3.  Look for more pairs to pick up.

4.  If the time comes when you have more cards on the table but you cannot find any pairs, the game is over.

5.  But if you pick up all the cards in pairs, you win the game and your wish will come true!

# ACES UP

### Get the Aces up and the rest of the cards will follow.

**Number of players:** One—it's a solitaire game.
**Object of game:** To get all the cards into four piles—one pile for each suit—in the "Places for Aces"

## SETTING UP THE GAME

♣ Lay out a row of seven cards *face down*. Leave room above for four "Places for Aces"

seven cards

♣ Put another card face down on top of each card.

fourteen cards

♣ Then lay down another row. This time do it *face up*. Lay the rest of the pack on the table face down. This is your stockpile. Now you are ready to play.

twenty-one cards

## THE PLACES FOR ACES

1. Look at the face-up cards. If you see any Aces, move them up to the Places for Aces. If any face-down cards are uncovered, turn them over.

2. Look at the cards again. If you see any 2's that match the Aces, move them up on top of the Aces. The 2 of Hearts goes on the Ace of Hearts, the 2 of Clubs goes on the Ace of Clubs, and so on. Then look for 3's, 4's, and so on. If you find any, move them up, too.

You've moved up the Ace of Spades. Turn over the card underneath. When you find the 2 of Spades, move it up on top of the Ace.

## BUILDING LADDERS

3. If you don't see any more cards to move up, look at your seven face-up cards again. You want to build "ladders" of cards that go down from the original seven. These ladders will have cards going from higher numbers to lower numbers. You always put a red card on a black card and a black card on a red card.

The suits don't matter here—only the colors and numbers are important. For example, a red 5 can be put only on a black 6. Then you can pick up the 5 and the 6 together and put them on a red 7.

## MOVING LADDERS

4. You have to move the whole ladder together. You cannot move just part of a ladder, and you cannot pull a card from the middle of the ladder. There is *one* card you *can* move by itself—the last card on the ladder. You can move it to another ladder, another pile, or to the Places for Aces.

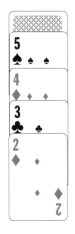

## TURNING THE STOCKPILE

5. When no more cards can be moved, turn over the first three cards in your stockpile and lay them in a pile on the table in front of you. Look at all the cards on the table. Can you put the top card on the Places for Aces or on one of your ladders?

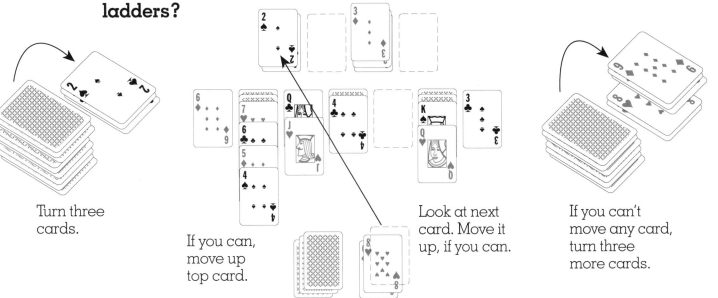

Turn three cards.

If you can, move up top card.

Look at next card. Move it up, if you can.

If you can't move any card, turn three more cards.

6. Keep going through the stockpile three cards at a time. When you finish, turn the pile over and start again.

7. **What happens when one of the seven piles becomes empty? You may put a King—by itself, or with its ladder—on the empty spot. If there is no King on the table, wait until one shows up as you play.**

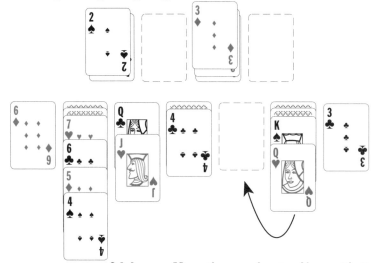

Is there an empty spot? Move a King there—by itself or with its ladder.

8. **If you move all the cards up to the Ace piles, you won! However, if the time comes when you keep going through the pack and find no more cards to move, the game is over, and you lost. Pick up all the cards, shuffle them, and set up for another game!**

## PLAYING ACES UP WITH TWO PLAYERS

1.  Two players sit at a table across from each other. Each player has her own deck of fifty-two cards. The backs of the cards must have different colors or patterns so you can tell them apart.

2.  Each player sets up her own layout, the same as in one-player Aces Up. Players leave room in the middle of the table for *eight* Places for Aces—four Aces from each deck.

3.  Each player follows the rules for one-player Aces Up. The only difference is that both players may put cards up on all eight Aces. It does not matter which Aces belong to which deck.

4.  When no more cards can be moved by either player, the game ends. Players turn over the Ace piles and separate their cards from their opponent's cards. Whoever has the most cards in the Places for Aces is the winner.

 **GO FISH**

## If you don't get the card you ask for, go fish for it.

**Number of players:** Two or more
**Object of game:** To get the most pairs of cards

♣ **A** *pair* **is any two cards that are the same.**

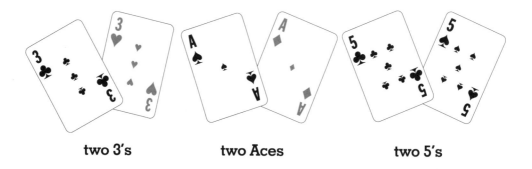

two 3's          two Aces          two 5's

1.  Shuffle and deal seven cards to each player. Put the rest of the deck face down in the center of the table. This is the *pick-up pile*.

2.  Players hold their cards in a fan and look at them. If a player has any pairs, she lays them face up in front of her.

3.  When everyone has finished looking at their cards, the first player may begin to ask other players for cards she needs to make pairs. For example, Fran might say, "Stan, do you have any 7's?" (Fran is not allowed to ask for a card she does not have in her hand.)

4. Stan looks for 7's. If he has any 7's, he *must* give one to Fran.

5. If Fran gets a 7, she then has a pair. She puts the pair of 7's face up on the table.

6. If Stan does *not* have a 7 in his hand, he tells Fran, "Go fish!"

7. Fran takes a card from the pick-up pile. If she gets the card she asked for, a 7, she lays down her pair and her turn continues. If she does not get the card she asked for, her turn ends. (If the card makes a pair with another card in her hand, she lays down the pair, but her turn still ends.)

8. Then it is the next player's turn.

9. If you ever run out of cards during the game, just take one from the pick-up pile when it's your turn.

10. When there are no cards left in the pick-up pile, the game ends. Players count up their pairs. Whoever has the most pairs wins.

If players tie, the one with the most groups of four cards wins. Below, each player has five pairs:

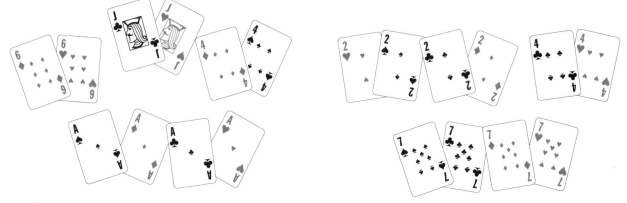

Five pairs, with one group of four.

Five pairs, with two groups of four. This player wins.

# WAR

## When two cards match—
## it's war!

**Number of players:** Best with two
**Object of game:** To get all the cards

1.  Shuffle and deal out all the cards.

2.  Each player holds his pack face down.

3.  Each player quickly lays his top card face up in the middle of the table.

4.  The player with the highest card takes both cards. He puts them on the bottom of his pack.

5.  If two matching cards come up—say, two 3's—it's war! (See "How to Fight a War" on page 22.)

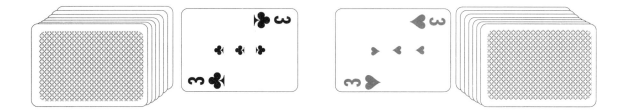

6.  The game ends when one player gets all the cards and is the winner.

## HOW TO FIGHT A WAR:

Each player puts three cards face down and one card face up on his own card. As the players lay the cards down, they say, "I declare war!"

The player with the higher card takes all the cards on the table. He turns them face down and adds them to the bottom of his pack.

## SOMETIMES IT'S DOUBLE WAR!

Sometimes when the players put down their cards for war, the last face-up cards are the same. Then they have to fight another war!

This time, both players put one war card face down and one card face up. The player with the highest card takes all the cards on the table.

The Ace wins!

 ## SNAP

Watch for cards that match,
then be the first to say, "Snap!"

**Number of players:** Good for two
**Object of game:** To get all the cards

1. Shuffle and deal out all the cards—including the Jokers.

2. Each player holds his pack face down.

3. Together the players say, "One, two, three." On the word *three*, the players quickly lay their top cards face up in the middle of the table.

4. If the cards do *not* match, the players repeat, "One, two, three" and lay down the next card.

5. If the cards match—two Kings, two 10's, two Aces—the first player to call out "Snap!" takes the cards.

She said "Snap" first. She takes the cards.

6. If both players call "Snap" at the same time, neither player takes the cards.

7. If you say "Snap" by mistake, you have to give one card to every player.

8. If one of the Jokers turns up, it's as good as a match. Again, the first player to call out "Snap!" takes the cards.

9. The player who gets all the cards is the winner.

# HELLO, SIR! HELLO, MISS!

In this game, you have to do some silly things
when special cards turn up.

**Number of players:** Best for two
**Object of game:** To get rid of all your cards

1.  Shuffle and deal out all the cards.

2.  Each player holds her pack face down.

3.  The first player lays her top card face up in the center of the
    table. (Don't peek as you turn the card over.)

4.  If the card on the table is a 2, 3, 4, 5, 6, 7, 8, or 9, the other
    player lays her top card on it.

5. If a "special" card turns up—a 10, a Jack, a Queen, a King, or an Ace—both players must quickly do these silly things:

10—wave your fingers

Jack—slap your own face
Gently, please!

Queen—say, "Hello, Miss!"

Hello, Miss!

Hello, Sir!

King—say, "Hello, Sir!"

Ace—touch your nose

6. The player who acts or speaks first, and does so correctly, does not have to pick up any cards. The other player must pick up all the cards on the table and add them to her pack.

7. Players take turns laying down cards. The first player to run out of cards is the winner.

It's fun to make up your own special cards and actions.

# *SPIT*

## In this game, you have to "spit" out cards fast!

**Number of players:** Best for two
**Object of game:** To get rid of all your cards

1. Shuffle and deal out all the cards.

2. Each player holds her pack face down.

3. Each player lays out four cards face up. These are the Table Cards.

4. Players chant together, "One, two, three—spit!" On the word *spit,* they each put down one card from their packs in the middle of the table. These will be the "Spit Piles."

Spit Piles                    Table Cards

5.     Now the game really begins. Players try to put as many Table Cards as they can onto the Spit Piles. *Both* players may put cards on *both* Spit Piles, but they must follow the rules below.

## RULES FOR PUTTING CARDS ON THE SPIT PILES

♣ Put a card that is *one higher* than the card on top of the Spit Pile. (A 3 can go on a 2, a 7 on a 6, a Queen on a Jack, and so on.)

♣ Put a card that is *one lower* than the card on top of the Spit Pile. (A 6 can go on a 7, a Queen on a King, and so on.)

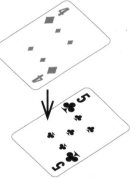

♣ In Spit, Aces are high *and* low. That means Aces may go on a King or on a 2!

♣ Suits don't matter—only numbers matter.

♣ You may not move two cards at the same time to a Spit Pile.

## RULES FOR THE TABLE CARDS

♣ Whenever you have fewer than four Table Cards, take cards from the top of your pack to fill in the empty places.

♣ If you have two cards of the same number, lay one on top of the other so that they take up only one space.

6. When neither player can put up any more Table Cards, the players again say, "One, two, three—spit!"

   On the word *spit*, they again lay a card from their packs in the middle of the table, and the game goes on.

7. When one player has no cards at all, or when neither player can put any more cards on the Spit Piles, then each player tries to slap the *smaller* Spit Pile.

   Whoever slaps it first takes it. The other player must take the bigger pile.

8. Each player shuffles all her cards. The players then lay out four new Table Cards and start the game again. Keep playing this way until one player has all the cards. The player with no cards is the winner.

You have to be fast!

SLAP!

# CONCENTRATION

Test your memory with this popular game.

**Number of players:** Two or more

**Object of game:** To take in the most pairs

1.  Shuffle the cards.

2.  Spread out all the cards face down.

3.  The first player turns any card face up and leaves it in the space where he found it. Then he turns a second card face up.

4.  If the two cards form a pair, the player gets to keep them and turn up two more cards.

I got a pair.

5. If the two cards do not make a pair, the player turns both cards face down again. Always put a card back in the very same spot.

6. Players try to remember where the cards are so they can find them again. For example, Sue turns over a 2 and a 3 and puts them face down again. Later, Lou turns over a 3. If he remembers where Sue's 3 was, he can turn it over and get a pair.

Now where was that other 3?

7. When all the cards have been taken, players count their cards. Whoever has the most wins.

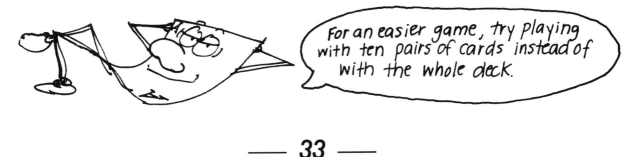

For an easier game, try playing with ten pairs of cards instead of with the whole deck.

# SLAPJACK

You have to be fast to play this game.
When you see a Jack—slap it!

**Number of players:** Two to six
**Object of game:** To get all the cards

1. Shuffle and deal out all the cards.

2. Each player puts his pack face down on the table in front of him.

3. The first player *quickly* puts his top card face up in the center of the table. When putting down cards, turn them fast and *do not peek!*

4. The next player puts his card face up on top of the first card, and so on.

Turn the cards over with one hand. Use the *other* hand to slap.

5. When a Jack is turned over, all the players try to slap their hand on it. The first player to slap the Jack wins the pile.

6. The next player then puts a new card out, and the game goes on as before.

7. If a player runs out of cards, he sits without playing until a Jack comes up. Then he tries to slap the Jack and get back in the game.

8. The winner is the one who ends up with all the cards.

# PIG

## Watch out, or you'll be the P-I-G!

**Number of players:** Three to thirteen
**Object of game:** To get four cards of the same suit and not become the Pig

### BEFORE THE GAME:

♣ Make a special deck with four cards of the same suit for each player. You will need paper and pencil for keeping score.

Sample deck for three players

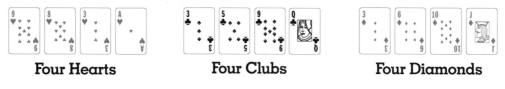

Four Hearts      Four Clubs      Four Diamonds

1.  Shuffle and deal out all the cards.

2.  Players hold cards in a fan.

3.  Players look at their cards. If anyone has four cards of the same suit, she puts her finger next to her nose.

4.  If no one has four cards of the same suit, the dealer says, "Go!" Each player passes one card face down to the player on her left.

5.  Repeat steps 3 and 4 until a player puts her finger next to her nose. As soon as she does, all the other players must do the same.

6.  The last player to put her finger next to her nose is the Pig.
    The other players point to the loser of the round and call
    out, "Pig!" and the pig must say, "Oink!"

7.  Start the game over again. The first time a player becomes
    the Pig, she must write a *p* on her score pad. The second
    time, she writes an *i*. Whoever spells out *pig* first loses the
    game and has to oink and snort like a pig.

**Helpful hint:** You have to keep an eye on your cards *and* on the other players. Do
you have four cards of the same suit? Is anyone holding a finger next to her nose?

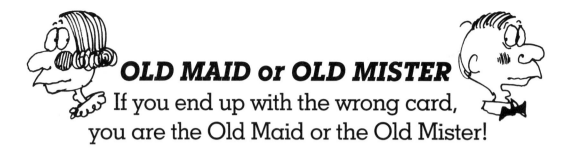

# OLD MAID or OLD MISTER

If you end up with the wrong card,
you are the Old Maid or the Old Mister!

**Number of players:** Three to six
**Object of game:** Not to get the Old Maid or Old Mister card

## BEFORE THE GAME:

♣ If you want to play Old Maid, take out all the Queens except the Queen of Spades. If you want to play Old Mister, take out all the Jacks except the Jack of Spades.

1. Shuffle and deal out all the cards. It doesn't matter if one player gets one card more or less than the others.

2. Hold your cards in a fan.

3. Each player looks for pairs in his hand. If he finds any, he lays them face up in a pile in front of him.

A pair is two matching cards.

4. The first player pulls one card—without looking at it—from the hand of the player to her left.

Just one!

5. Then the first player looks to see if she can make a pair with the new card. If she can, she lays the pair down.

6. The next player pulls one card from the player to his left. This continues until all pairs have been laid down.

A pair!

7. One player will be left with the Queen or the Jack. That player is the Old Maid or the Old Mister and loses the game.

I'm the Old Mister!

# *MY SHIP SAILS*

In this game, you win when all your cards
are the same suit.

**Number of players:** Four or more
**Object of game:** To get any seven cards of the same suit, for example:

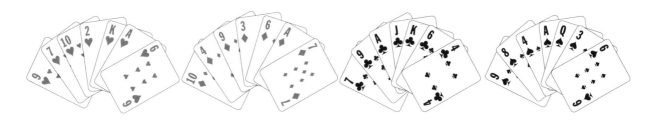

seven Hearts          seven Diamonds          seven Clubs          seven Spades

♣ Pay attention to suits in this game.

1. Shuffle and deal seven cards to each player. Put the rest of
   the deck aside. You will not need it.

2. Hold your cards in a fan. Arrange them by suit—put all the
   Hearts together, all the Clubs together, and so on. Don't
   worry if you don't have all the suits.

Lay aside the rest of the deck.

3. Each player passes one card face down to the player on his left. (See "Tips for Passing Cards" on page 42.)

4. When all the cards have been passed, everyone picks his card up at the same time. Each player puts the new card in his hand next to others of the same suit.

5. Then everyone passes a card again.

6. The game goes on until one player gets seven cards of the same suit. That player calls out, "My ship sails!" He is the winner.

## TIPS FOR PASSING CARDS:

**Keep cards when you have several others of the same suit. Pass cards when you have few cards of the same suit. Try to pass a "lone" card if you have one.**

Pass the 3 of Diamonds. It's a lone card.

Pass either one of the lone cards.

You have three Diamonds but only *two* Hearts and *two* Spades.
Keep the Diamonds. Pass any other card.

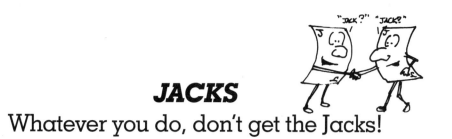

# *JACKS*
## Whatever you do, don't get the Jacks!

**Number of players:** Best with four
**Object of game:** Not to get any Jacks

## BEFORE THE GAME:
♣ Take away all cards lower than 7 so that you are playing
with only the thirty-two highest cards—all of the 7's, 8's, 9's,
10's, Jacks, Queens, Kings, and Aces. You will need paper
and pencil for keeping score.

Take these out of the deck.

Use these.

1.  Shuffle and deal out all the cards.

2.  The first player lays one card face up in the center of the
    table. Everyone must notice the suit of that card—is it a
    Heart, Diamond, Spade, or Club?

3. Each of the other players must then lay down a card of that suit. For example, if the first player put down a Heart, the other players must also put down a Heart if they have one. If a player has no cards of the original suit in her hand, she may lay down a card of another suit.

4. The player who puts out the highest card of the *original* suit takes all the cards. If there is only one card of the original suit, then that card wins.

5.  The player who won the last hand lays down the next card face up, and the game goes on as before.

6.  When all the cards have been played, the players look through their cards and pull out any Jacks.

7.  Each Jack counts *against* the player—the Jack of Spades counts three points; the others count one point. Write down each player's score.

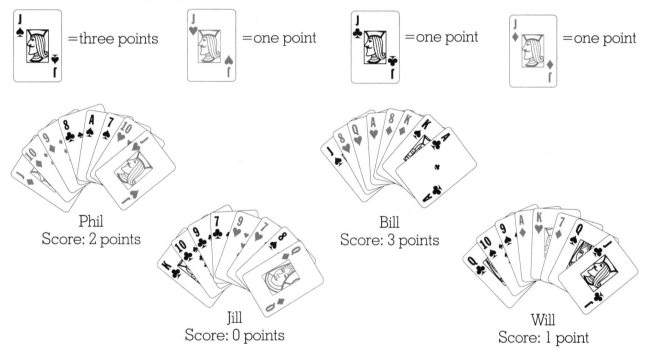

J♠ =three points    J♥ =one point    J♣ =one point    J♦ =one point

Phil
Score: 2 points

Jill
Score: 0 points

Bill
Score: 3 points

Will
Score: 1 point

8.  Shuffle and deal the cards again. Play another round and write down the scores. Do this until one player gets ten points. That player is the loser. The winner is the one with the *fewest* points.

# *I DOUBT IT*

Players tell what cards they have.
But are they telling the truth? You may doubt it.

**Number of players:** Three or more
**Object of game:** To get rid of all your cards

1. Shuffle and deal out all the cards so everyone has the same number. If any cards are left over, put them face down in the center of the table.

2. Players hold their cards in a fan. Suits don't matter in this game.

3. The first player picks one, two, three, or four cards from her hand and lays them face down. She says, "Here are two Aces," or "This is one Ace," or whatever. The first player must say she has Aces, but she does *not* have to tell the truth! She could say, "Two Aces," but put down two 7's, or a 7 and a King. She can also put down an Ace and any other card.

4.  Now the other players decide if they believe the first player. If any player does not, he calls out, "I doubt it!"

5.  If a player says, "I doubt it," the cards are turned over.

    If the first player was telling the truth, the doubter must add the cards to *his* hand. He must also take any other cards on the table.

    If the first player was not telling the truth, she must put the cards—*and* any others on the table—back in her hand.

    If no one says, "I doubt it," the cards stay on the table and it is the next player's turn.

    If two or more players say, "I doubt it" at the very same time, the one who is closest to the first player's left is the official doubter. If he is wrong, he is the one who must put the cards in his hand.

6. Now the second player puts down some cards and says, "These are four 2's," or "three 2's," or "two 2's," or "one 2." The second player must say he has 2's, but he does not have to put 2's down.

7. The game goes on as before. The third player says, "3's," and so on. When you finish with Kings, start over with Aces. When it is his turn, each player must put down at least one card.

8. The first player to get rid of all his cards is the winner.

**Helpful hint:** Sometimes you can tell if another player is not telling the truth. Just compare your cards with what he says.

# STEAL THE PACK

It's okay to take someone else's pack
in this exciting game.

**Number of players:** Best with two, three, or four
**Object of game:** To take the most cards

1. Shuffle and deal four cards to each player. Lay four cards face up in the center of the table. These are called the Table Cards. The dealer keeps the rest of the deck to use later.

2. Players hold their cards in a fan. Suits don't matter in this game—only numbers are important.

3. In turn, players make plays to pick up cards, which they place face up next to them in a pack. You may not make a play unless it is your turn. You may *not* take cards or steal a pack between turns.

Table Cards

Dealer's deck

Players can make the following plays:

♣ Take one of the Table Cards by matching it with a card in your hand. Place *both* cards face up in a pack next to you.

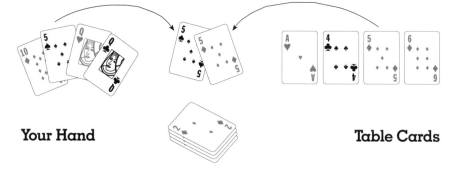

Your Hand · Table Cards

♣ If there are two or three cards of the same kind on the table, you may take them. Place all matching cards in your pack.

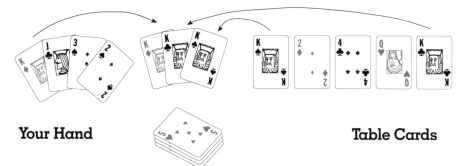

Your Hand · Table Cards

♣ Take another player's pack with a card that matches the card on the top of her pack.

4.  If a player cannot take any cards, she must take a card from her hand and lay it next to the Table Cards.

5.  When all the players have used all four cards in their hands, the dealer deals out four more cards to each one. He does not deal any more cards to the table, however.

6.  The last player to take any cards from the table gets all the cards that are left.

7.  The player who has the most cards is the winner.

# CRAZY EIGHTS

You'll love the eights
in this game—they're wild!

**Number of players:** Three or more
**Object of game:** To get rid of all your cards

1.  Shuffle and deal seven cards to each player. Place the deck face down in the middle of the table. This is the pick-up pile. Turn one card face up next to the pile. This is the throw-away pile.

2.  Players hold their cards in a fan and arrange them by suits—the Hearts together, the Clubs together, and so on.

3. The first player has to lay a card on top of the face-up card. This card has to be of the *same suit*—a Club on a Club, a Heart on a Heart, and so on.

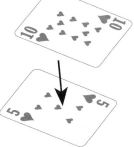

4. If you want to change suits, you can lay down a card of the *same number*—a 10 of Spades on a 10 of Hearts, for example. The next player must then put down a card of the new suit.

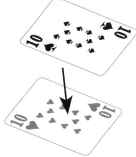

5. Eights are "wild"—that is, you may put down an 8 anytime and call out *any suit you wish*. It does not have to be the suit of the 8.

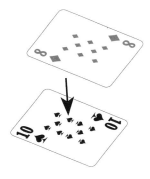

6. **If you have no matching cards and no 8's, you must draw cards from the pick-up pile until you find one you can lay down.**

7. **When the pick-up pile runs out, turn the throw-away pile face down to make a new one. (Don't forget to shuffle it!)**

8. **The first player to lay down all her cards is the winner.**

**Helpful hints:** Notice which suits have been put down. For example, if a lot of Diamonds have been played and you still have Diamonds in your hand, try to change the suit to Diamonds.

Eights are very valuable. Don't waste them. Use 8's to stop someone who is close to winning, or to change the suit if that will help you win.

For a quicker, easier game, deal out only five cards to each player.

# BEGINNING RUMMY

When you're down to one card,
it's time to say, "Rummy!"

**Number of players:** Good for two players; can also be played by three, four, or five
**Object of game:** To get rid of your cards

1. Shuffle and deal each player ten cards. Place the deck face down in the middle of the table. This will be the pick-up pile. Turn over one card next to it. This will be the throw-away pile.

2. Players hold their cards in a fan.

3. In turn, each player tries to lay a group of three cards face up on the table. You may lay cards in these two patterns:

♣ **TRIPLET**

Three matching cards.

♣ **RUN**

Three cards of the same suit in order.

The Ace may be used before the 2 as a low card or after the King as a high card, but you cannot use it *both* ways at the same time. That is, you may *not* have K, A, 2.

4.  To begin the game, the first player looks at the face-up card in the throw-away pile. If he can use it to make a triplet or a run, he picks it up and lays down his triplet or run on the table in front of him. If a player takes the face-up card, he must use it *at once*. He may not save it.

5.  If the player cannot use the face-up card, he draws the top card from the pick-up pile.

6.  He looks at his hand. If he has a triplet or a run, he lays it on the table in front of him.

7.  If a player does not have a triplet or run, he may add to one that is already on the table. (It may be his own or another player's.)  For example, if there are three 6's down and he has a 6 in his hand, he may lay it next to the other 6's.

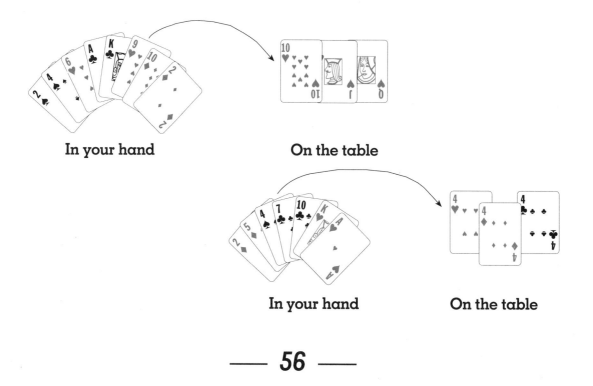

In your hand                    On the table

In your hand                    On the table

8. During each turn, you may lay down only one card or one group of three cards. If you hold four cards in a group or run, you may not put them all down in the same turn. On your first turn, you may put down three cards. You must wait until another turn to lay down the fourth card.

9. At the end of your turn, you must throw away one card face up on the throw-away pile.

10. When one player has used all her cards except one, she can "go out." She slaps her card face down on the throw-away pile and calls out, "Rummy!" She is the winner.

11. If all the cards in the pick-up pile are used up before the game is over, the throw-away pile is turned face down and becomes the new pick-up pile.

# *TWENTY-ONE*
## Try to reach twenty-one, but don't go over!

**Number of players:** Two to seven
**Object of game:** To get a hand of cards in which all the numbers add up to twenty-one—or as close as possible to twenty-one *without* going over it

## WHAT THE CARDS ARE WORTH:

**FACE CARDS**= ten

**ACE**= **one or eleven** (it can be either; you decide when you see your cards)

**NUMBER CARDS**= face value

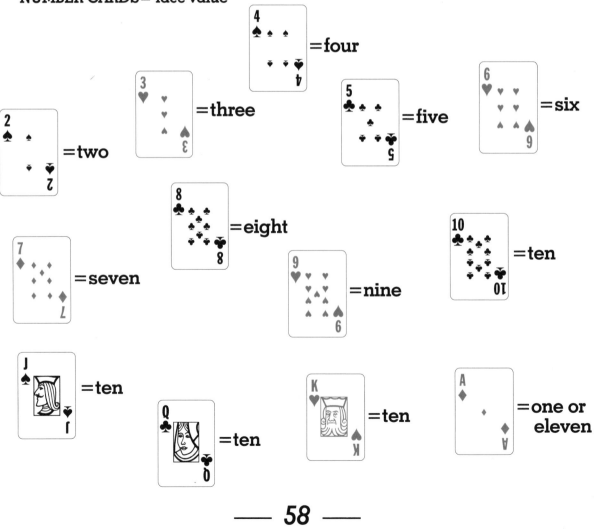

1. The dealer gives each player—including herself—one card *face down*.

2. The dealer gives everyone a second card. This time, it is *face up*.

3. First, look at your face-up card. Then peek at your face-down card. (Don't let anyone else see it!) Add your two cards together.

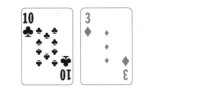

thirteen

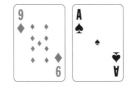

twenty or ten, Ace = 1 or 11

4. If your hand adds up to less than twenty-one, you have a chance to ask for more cards. You say, "Hit me," and the dealer gives you another card face down. Then you add up your cards again. If they are still under twenty-one, you may say, "Hit me" again.

5. Each player gets a turn to ask for as many cards as she wants. If you are very close to twenty-one but still under, you might want to tell the dealer, "No more cards!" Another card might make you go over twenty-one. You have to decide how much of a chance you want to take!

6. If your hand adds up to twenty-one, tell the dealer you don't want any cards. If you do go over twenty-one, show your cards and say, "I'm busted."

7. When everyone has been dealt new cards, players who are still in the game take turns showing their hands. Whoever gets twenty-one (or the closest number under twenty-one) wins the game. In this game, there can be more than one winner.

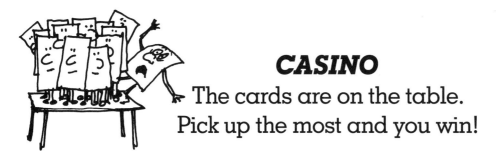

# CASINO

The cards are on the table.
Pick up the most and you win!

**Number of players:** Best with two, three, or four players
**Object of game:** To take the most cards

♣ Aces always equal 1.

1. Shuffle and deal four cards to each player. Lay four cards face up on the table. These are the Table Cards.

2. Players hold their cards in a fan. Suits don't matter in this game!

3. Players take turns picking up cards from the table by using any of the following plays: Matching, Combining, Calling, and Building.

Remember, the first player is always to the left of the dealer.

## MATCHING:

Take one or more of the Table Cards by matching it with a card in your hand. You may play *only* one card from your hand on each turn.

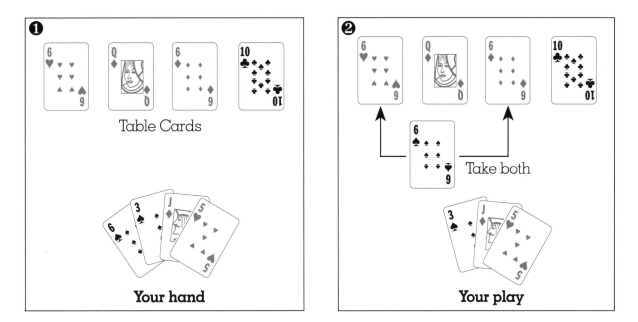

Table Cards

Your hand

Take both

Your play

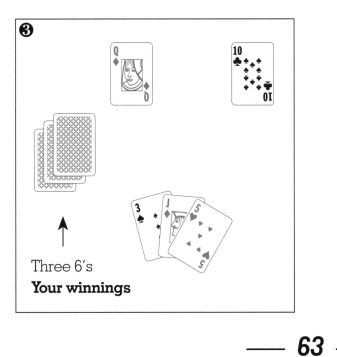

Three 6's
**Your winnings**

## COMBINING:

Take two or more of the Table Cards that *add up to* a card in your hand. Sometimes there is more than one combination that adds up to the card in your hand. For example, 2 plus 4 equal 6 and 1 plus 3 plus 2 equal 6. You can pick up both combinations on the same turn.

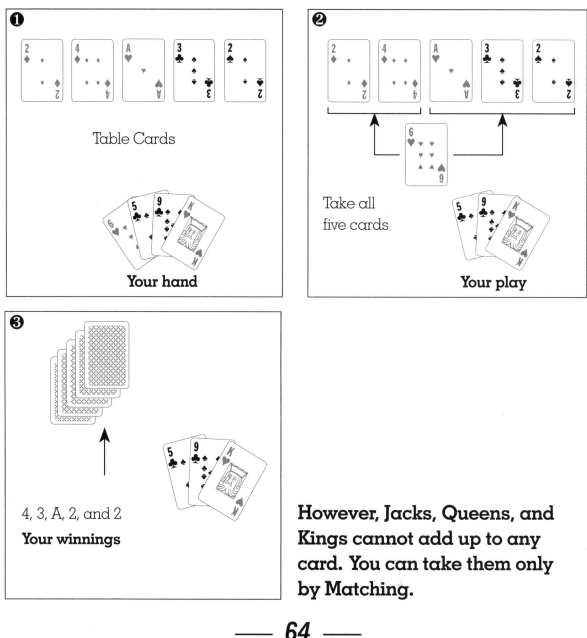

**❶**

Table Cards

**Your hand**

**❷**

Take all
five cards

**Your play**

**❸**

4, 3, A, 2, and 2

**Your winnings**

However, Jacks, Queens, and Kings cannot add up to any card. You can take them only by Matching.

## CALLING:

Calling takes more than one turn because you have to use more than one card from your hand. Sometimes, Calling is like Matching. For example, you have two 3's in your hand. On the table is one 3, and you want to use both of your 3's to pick up the 3 on the table. Here's how to do it:

Lay one 3 on top of the 3 on the table and call the play by saying, "Threes." On your next turn, take the pile with your second 3.  However, if another player has a 3, he can take the pile before you do!

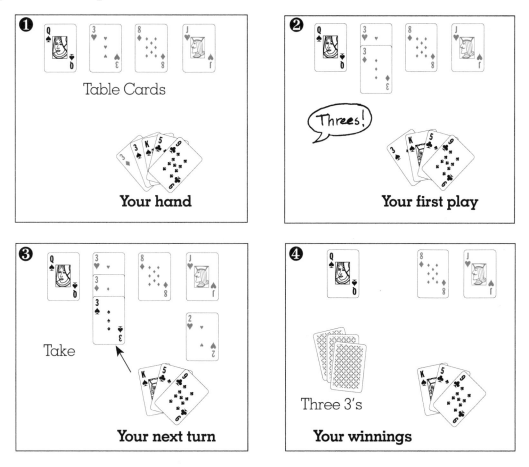

① Table Cards / Your hand

② Threes! / Your first play

③ Take / Your next turn

④ Three 3's / Your winnings

Other times, Calling is like Combining. You have two 7's in your hand. There are a 6 and an Ace on the table. Put the 6 and the Ace together, lay your 7 on top of them, and call, "Sevens." On your next turn, pick up the whole pile with your other 7.

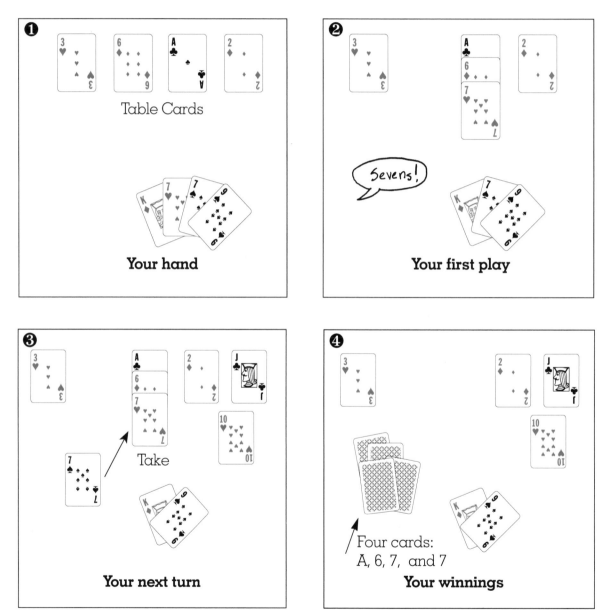

Notice how the cards on the table change. That is because players are picking up and putting down cards with each turn.

## BUILDING:

Suppose there is a 6 on the table and you have a 2 and an 8 in your hand. You want to arrange things so you can take the 2 and the 6 with your 8. You do it by building. Here's how:

On your first turn, lay your 2 on the 6 and say, "Building 8's." On your next turn, pick up the cards with your 8. But remember that another player may pick up the cards with an 8, too!

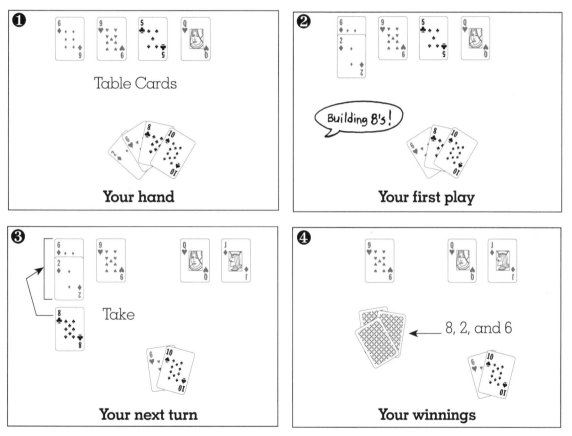

Another player may add to the pile that you are building and make it a higher number. For instance, if you have a pile of 8's, another player may lay down a 2 and say, "Building 10's." Then she or any other player—including you!—may pick up the pile on the next turn if that person has a 10.

4. If a player is not able to take any Table Cards, she must discard. To do this, she lays down a card face up from her hand in the center of the table.

5. Each time the players have played all four cards in their hands, the dealer deals out four more cards to each one. The dealer does not deal any more cards to the table. Table Cards are replaced by players discarding.

6. The person who makes *the last play to take cards* picks up all the remaining cards on the table.

7. Here are two ways to win Casino:

♣ Count your cards. Whoever has the most cards is the winner.

♣ To make things a little more interesting, you can play Casino for points. Here's how to keep score:

> MOST CARDS....3 points
> MOST SPADES....1 point
> 10 OF DIAMONDS (also called "Big Casino")....2 points
> 2 OF SPADES (also called "Little Casino")....1 point
> EACH ACE....1 point

The player with the most points is the winner.

# *POKER*

In this favorite game, the highest hand wins.
Here's a simple way to play.

**Number of players:** Two to ten, but best for four to seven
**Object of game:** To get the hand with the highest Poker combinations in it (see pages 72–73)

1. **Shuffle and deal five cards to each player.**

2. **Hold your cards in a fan.**

3. **Look at your cards and arrange them into the Poker combinations described on pages 72–73. If you have two cards that match, for instance, put them together in your hand to make a pair. If you have three cards in order, put them together, and so on.**

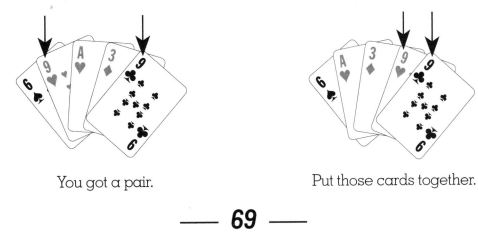

You got a pair.                    Put those cards together.

4. **Now you can get some new cards from the dealer. When it is your turn, lay down the cards you do *not* want and ask for the same number of new cards. For example, if you have a pair and the other three cards in your hand do not look promising, lay them down and ask for three new cards.**

Keep the pair. Lay down the rest.

5. **Look at your cards again. Arrange your hand again.**

You got another 9!

Put the new 9 with the other two.

6. Each player shows his hand. The player with the highest Poker combinations wins. If no one has any combinations, the person with the highest card wins.

# THE POKER HANDS FROM LOWEST TO HIGHEST

Each player is dealt five cards. To win, you need certain combinations of cards in your hand. Before you play, study the nine Poker combinations below. As you play, you will learn them by heart.

### ♣ ONE PAIR
Two matching cards. It doesn't matter what the other cards are.

### ♣ TWO PAIRS
Two sets of matching cards.

### ♣ THREE OF A KIND
Three matching cards.

### ♣ STRAIGHT
Five cards in order, but *not* all the same suit.

*In a straight, Aces may be high or low.*

## ♣ FLUSH

Five cards of the same suit, but not in order.

## ♣ FULL HOUSE

Three of a kind plus one pair—in any suits.

## ♣ FOUR OF A KIND

Four matching cards.

## ♣ STRAIGHT FLUSH

Any five cards in the same suit *and* in order.

## ♣ ROYAL FLUSH

The 10, Jack, Queen, King, and Ace,
all in the same suit.

# BREAKING A TIE IN POKER

When players have the same kind of hand, whoever has the highest cards wins. Aces are high, except when they are used as 1's in a straight.

**TWO PAIRS**

Pair of Aces. This hand wins.

**THREE OF A KIND**

Higher cards. This hand wins.

**FLUSH**

King is high card. This hand wins.

**STRAIGHT**

Higher cards. This hand wins.

Ace is 1 here.

**What if two hands are *exactly the same*? Then you must look at the suits. Hearts are highest, then Spades, then Diamonds, and Clubs are lowest.**

**Both hands are straight flushes.**

Hearts are highest. This hand wins.

**Both hands are straights.**

The high card is a Diamond.

The high card is a Spade. Spades are higher than Diamonds. This hand wins.

# WHERE TO FIND MORE

## SOME SOURCES FOR CARD GAMES

Collis, Len. *Card Games for Children.* New York: Barron's, 1989.

Editors of Klutz Press. *The Klutz Book of Card Games for Sharks and Others.* Palo Alto, California: Klutz Press, 1990.

Leeming, Joseph. *Games and Fun with Playing Cards.* New York: Dover Publications, 1949.

MacColl, Gail. *The Book of Cards for Kids.* New York: Workman Publishing, 1992.

Morehead, Albert H. *Official Rules of Card Games.* New York: Fawcett Crest, 1990.

Street, Michael. *Lucky Thirteen: Solitaire Games for Kids.* New York: SeaStar Books, 2001.